Cause

Effect

Chaos!

Space

Author Paul Mason
with artwork by Mark Ruffle

Enslow PUBLISHING

The website addresses (URLs) included in this book were valid at the time of going to press. However, it is possible that contents or addresses may have changed since the publication of this book. No responsibility for any such change can be accepted by either the author or the Publisher.

Published in 2026 by Enslow Publishing, LLC
2544 Clinton Street
Buffalo, NY 14224

First published in Great Britain in 2018 by Wayland

Series editor: Paul Rockett
Series design and illustration: Mark Ruffle
www.rufflebrothers.com

Manufactured in the United States of America

CPSIA compliance information: Batch #CSENS26: For further information contact Enslow Publishing LLC, New York, New York at 1-800-398-2504.

Please visit our website, www.enslowpublishing.com. For a free color catalog of all our high-quality books, call toll free 1-800-398-2504 or fax 1-877-980-4454.

Cataloging-in-Publication Data
Names: Mason, Paul. | Ruffle, Mark, illustrator.
Title: Space / Paul Mason ; illustrated by Mark Ruffle.
Description: Buffalo, NY : Enslow Publishing, 2026. |
Series: Cause, effect, chaos! | Includes glossary and index.
Identifiers: ISBN 9781978545298 (pbk.) | ISBN 9781978545304 (library bound) |
ISBN 9781978545311 (ebook)
Subjects: LCSH: Outer space--Juvenile literature. | Astronomy--Juvenile literature. | Astronautics in astronomy--Juvenile literature.
Classification: LCC QB500.22 M376 2026 | DDC 520--dc23

Contents

Cause and Effect 4

Solar Flare! 6

When the Sun Goes Out 8

Meteorite Mayhem! 10

Mission to the Moon 12

Space Life 14

Pee in Zero-G 16

Lost in Space! 18

Mars: Planet of War! 20

Risky Ride to Neptune 22

Death of a Star 24

Great Balls of Fire! 26

Galactic Cannibals 28

Glossary 30

Finding Out More 31

Index 32

Cause and Effect

What causes events to happen? Usually they are the effect of something that happened just before.

You can probably think of a few examples from your own life:

You study hard

at school, or you train hard at gymnastics, football, or ballet.

You get a good grade, or finally do a backflip, score a goal, or perform a perfect pirouette.

Of course, not every action has a good effect:

You "borrow" your mom's iPad and accidentally download a paid-for app.

No allowance for a month.

Chaos with your social plans! No more movies or shopping trips.

Down here on Earth, cause and effect is sometimes painful–and sometimes even deadly. So just imagine what things are like in **OUTER SPACE!**

The Earth is slowly moving further from the sun.

If Earth moves too far away, we will lose the sun's heat. Everyone will freeze to death!

Fortunately, big events in outer space happen slowly. For example, we are only moving 6 inches (15 cm) from the sun each year. It will be a very long time before this is a problem.

Solar Flare!

Most humans feel happy on a sunny day. No wonder–like every other living thing, we actually need sunshine to survive.

Sunshine is a kind of energy that comes from the sun, the star at the center of our solar system.

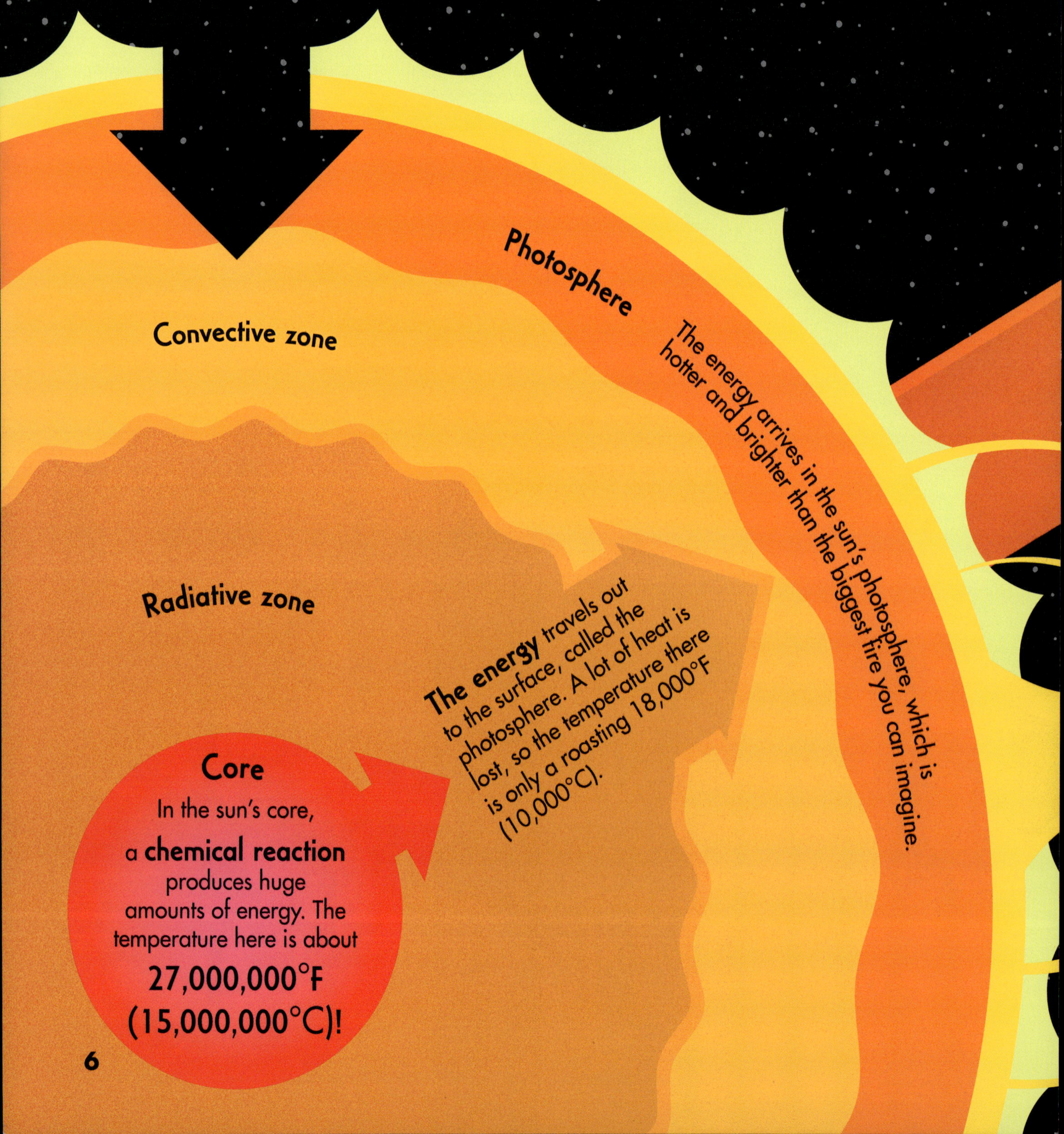

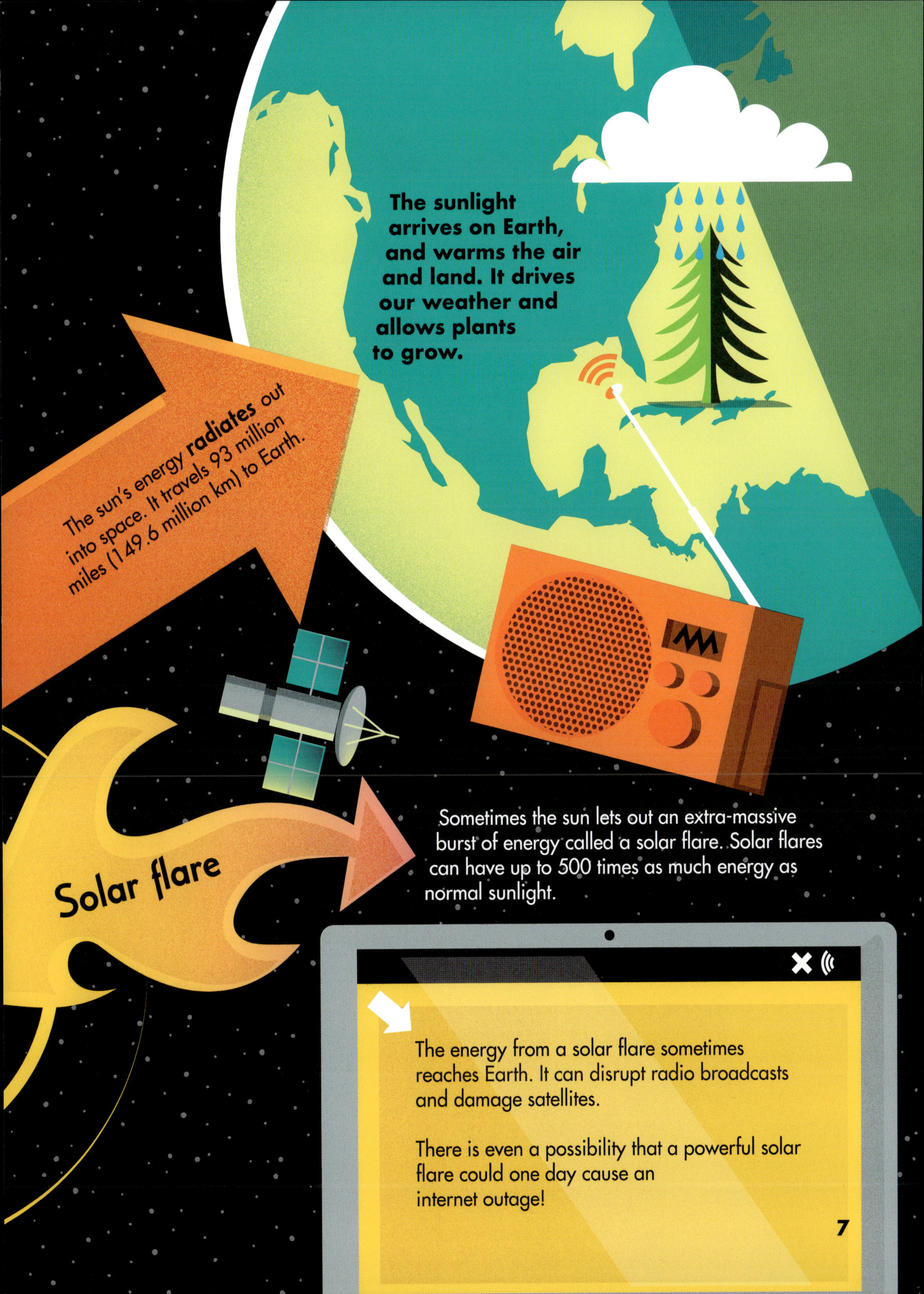

The sun's energy **radiates** out into space. It travels 93 million miles (149.6 million km) to Earth.

The sunlight arrives on Earth, and warms the air and land. It drives our weather and allows plants to grow.

Sometimes the sun lets out an extra-massive burst of energy called a solar flare. Solar flares can have up to 500 times as much energy as normal sunlight.

The energy from a solar flare sometimes reaches Earth. It can disrupt radio broadcasts and damage satellites.

There is even a possibility that a powerful solar flare could one day cause an internet outage!

When the Sun Goes Out

Without sunshine, plants would not grow and there would be no weather or seasons. Planet Earth would be just another cold, dark rock traveling through space.

Two celestial bodies move through our sky in daytime:

the **sun and the moon.**
The moon moves slowly, the sun often catches up with it.

Sometimes as the sun catches up it goes behind the moon. When it is partly behind, there is a strange half-light down on Earth.*

*The sun is 400 times wider than the moon. They appear the same size because the sun is also 400 times further away.

If the **sun** goes right behind the moon, its light is blocked out completely. This is called

a total eclipse.

A giant shadow 100 miles (160 km) across falls on the Earth's surface. At the heart of the shadow it is suddenly like nighttime.

A total eclipse happens somewhere on Earth about every 18 months.

This sudden darkness tricks animals into thinking night has come.

Birds rush to their nests. Nighttime insects start chirping and tweeting. Spiders start taking down their webs. There are even reports that hippos get scared and hide underwater!

Meteorite Mayhem!

When you look up into the nighttime sky, you might see what looks like a star shooting through space. It's actually a meteor heading towards the Earth!

A meteor begins life as a **meteoroid** –a piece of space rock that has come away from an asteroid or comet.

When it falls into the Earth's atmosphere it becomes a meteor.

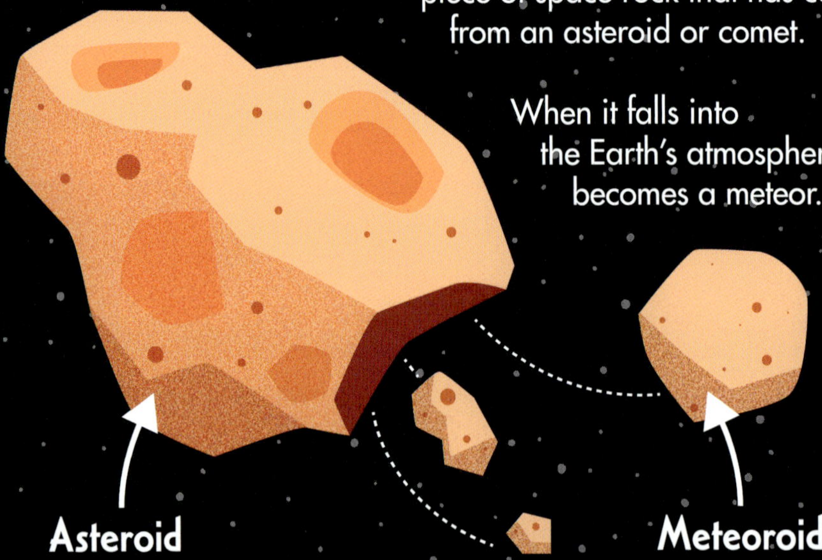

As the meteor falls, friction between the rock and gases in Earth's atmosphere causes it to heat up and glow. This is what makes the meteor visible.

Several meteors all falling towards Earth at the same time are called a **meteor shower**.

Most meteors burn up and become dust before they can hit the Earth's surface.

Space dust from meteors falls to Earth every day.

A meteor that hits the Earth is called a

meteorite.

Some scientists think that 65 million years ago a 6.2-mile (10-km) wide meteorite hit the Earth, causing massive dust clouds, fires, and tsunamis. They believe this caused the dinosaurs to become extinct.

Mission to the Moon

In 1969, three astronauts went to the moon. Their mission was called Apollo 11.

The astronauts were Buzz Aldrin, Neil Armstrong, and Michael Collins. No one was sure if they could reach the moon–or make it home again alive.

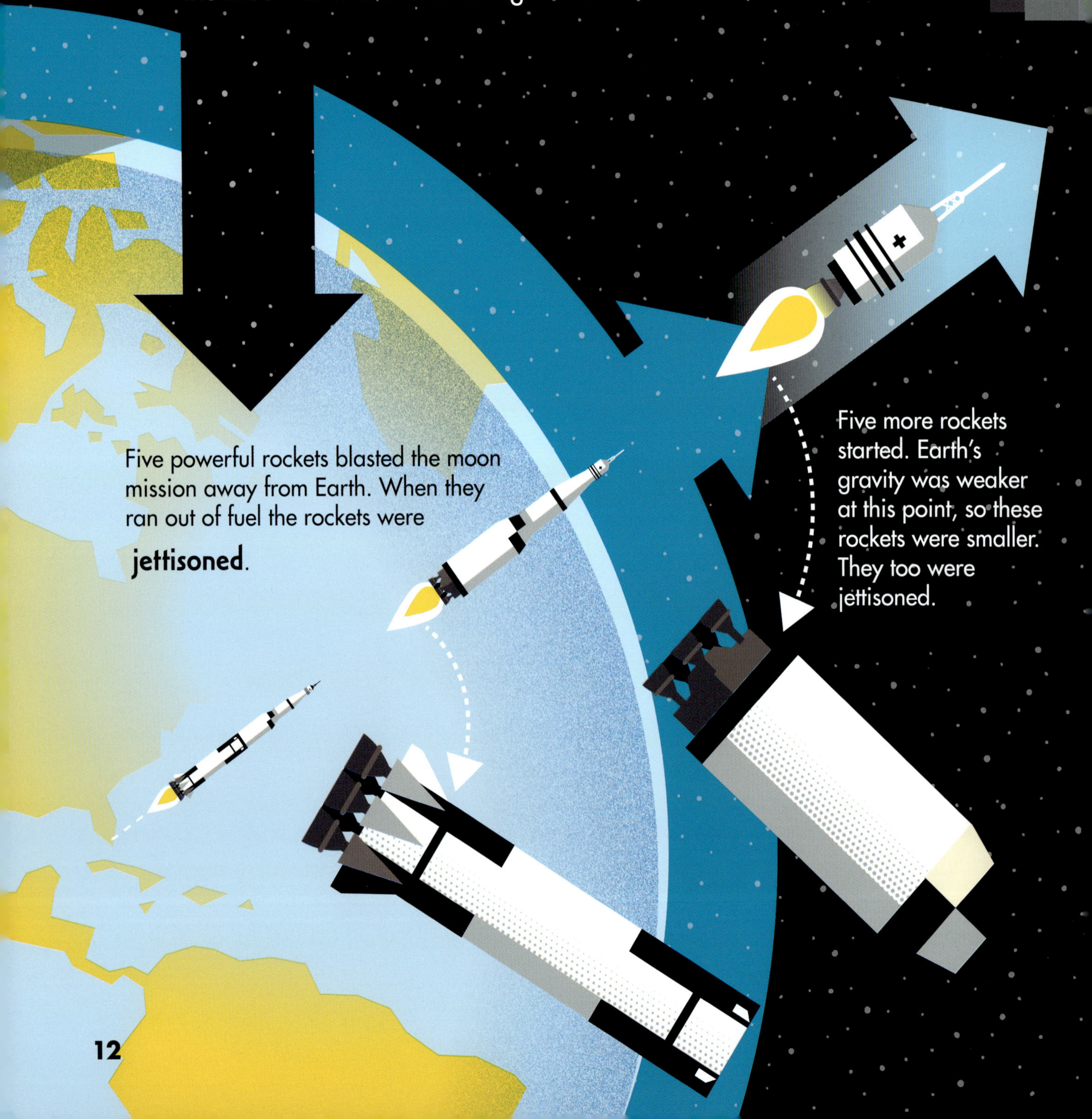

Five powerful rockets blasted the moon mission away from Earth. When they ran out of fuel the rockets were **jettisoned**.

Five more rockets started. Earth's gravity was weaker at this point, so these rockets were smaller. They too were jettisoned.

The spacecraft now had one main rocket left. This fired it towards the moon's orbit. When it arrived, Aldrin and Armstrong got into the Lunar Module.

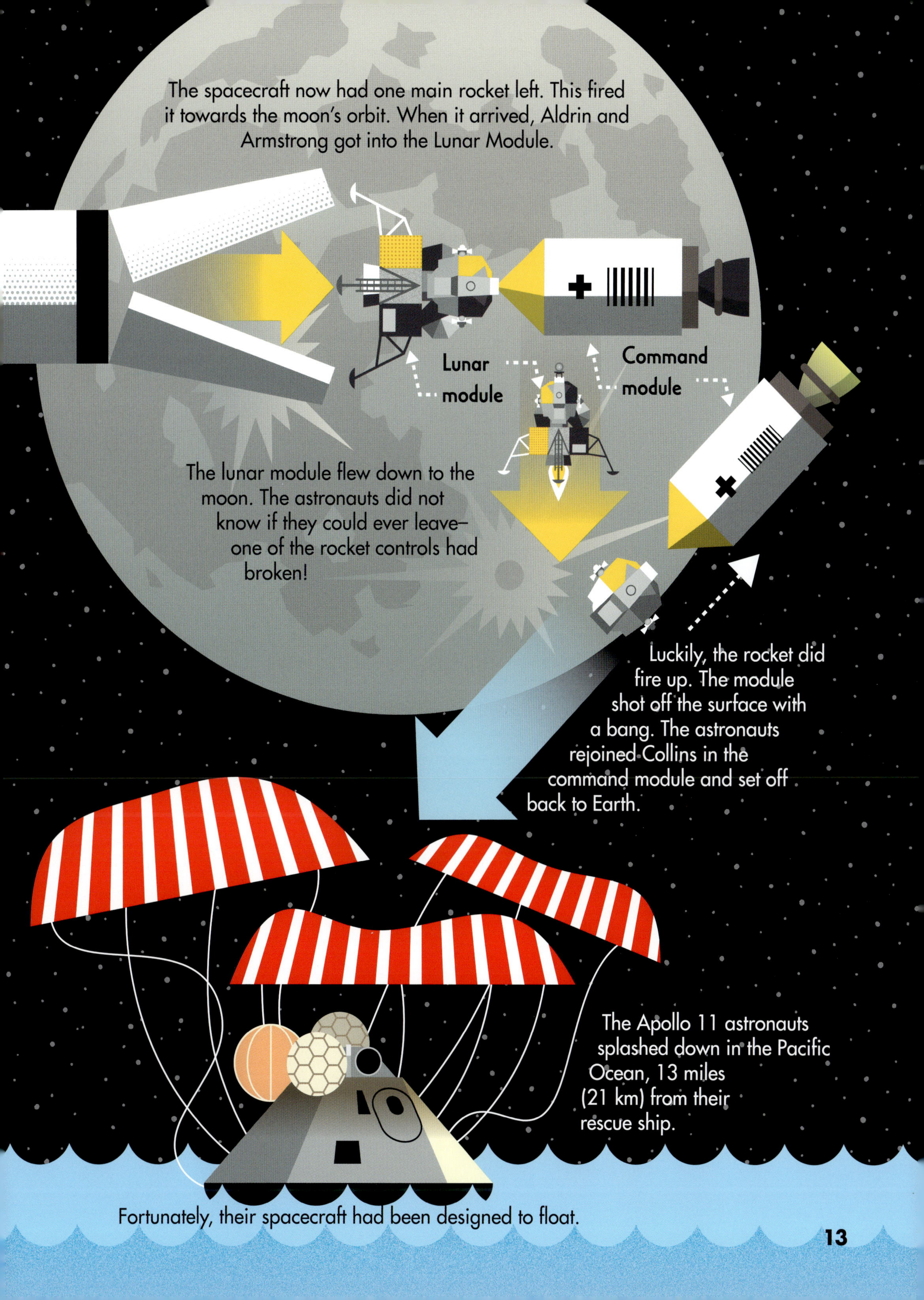

The lunar module flew down to the moon. The astronauts did not know if they could ever leave– one of the rocket controls had broken!

Luckily, the rocket did fire up. The module shot off the surface with a bang. The astronauts rejoined Collins in the command module and set off back to Earth.

The Apollo 11 astronauts splashed down in the Pacific Ocean, 13 miles (21 km) from their rescue ship.

Fortunately, their spacecraft had been designed to float.

Space Life

Astronauts last visited the moon in 1972, though future missions are planned. But, they have spent time living in space! The record is 437 days* in space–well over a year!

Our bodies are designed for living with Earth's gravity, but in space there is no gravity. So, what effect does living in space have on a human?

On the **space station** there is no gravity to help blood flow downwards. Instead, extra blood stays in the upper body and head. The astronauts' faces quickly become puffy.

When the spacecraft blasts off, some astronauts feel nauseous as the launch vehicle climbs into Earth's atmosphere.

With **extra blood** in their upper bodies, there is less in the astronauts' legs. Their legs shrink, becoming wrinkled and thin.

*Set by Valeri Polyakov, from January 1994 to March 1995.

Fortunately, exercising while aboard the space station helps astronauts stay healthy.

When they get back to

Earth's gravity,

their bodies do recover.

When bones lose density, they break more easily. Just knocking into something can break an arm or leg!

Because the astronauts never stand up, there is less stress on their leg bones. Their bones become weaker. They lose 1 percent of their bone density per month.

Unkind observers call this

"chicken-leg syndrome."

Pee in Zero-G

Aboard a space station, gravity does not pull you downwards as it does on Earth. You actually feel zero gravity—often called zero-G.

With zero-G, everything that isn't fixed in place just floats off! Even simple activities become complicated. Activities like putting ketchup on food, spitting out toothpaste, washing … and peeing …

First, the astronaut switches on a fan at the end of a long, flexible pipe. The fan sucks air into the pipe.

Now the astronaut pees—with the pipe VERY close by. Otherwise the pee just floats off!

Once enough has been collected, the pee is heated to boiling point and turns to steam.

The pee-steam container spins around at high speed. Any contaminants are pressed against the side of the container. The pure steam stays in the middle.

Aboard the International Space Station, American astronauts don't just collect pee from their own side of the station. They also collect pee from the Russian side. The Russians don't want their pee, so they let the Americans have it.

Pee is sucked into the space station's Urine Processing Assembly, or UPA. It is about 95 percent water. The astronauts need the water, which is a valuable resource, back!

The steam is cooled down and turns back into liquid.

If the process has worked, the pee becomes clean water for thirsty astronauts to drink. If it hasn't, they get a nasty surprise!

Lost in Space!

Sometimes astronauts go outside a space station. Space experts call this an "extra vehicular activity" or EVA. Most people call it a space walk.

A space walk begins when the astronaut goes outside through an air lock.

The inner door is closed, to keep air inside the space station. Then the outer door is opened and the astronaut climbs out.

The astronaut clips on a safety tether, or a line attaching them to the space station.

If the astronaut accidentally pushes away from the space station, the tether means they are still attached to the space station.

If the tether breaks, the astronaut sails off into space.

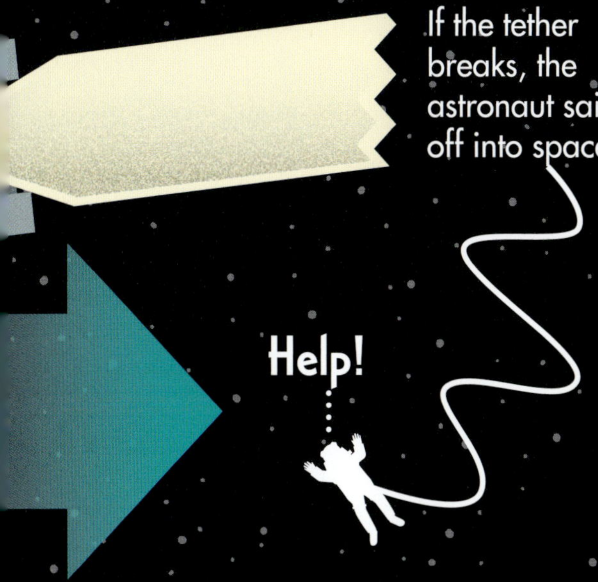

They will either:

a) run out of oxygen and water, resulting in death, or;

b) be sucked into Earth's gravity and burn up like a meteor, resulting in death.

So, the astronaut turns on the

jet pack on the space suit!

Once the jet pack is on, the astronaut uses a hand-held controller–like a video-game joystick–to rocket back to safety.

The jet packs only have a small amount of fuel–but it is enough to get back to the space station or rescue someone else who has come untethered.

Mars: Planet of War!

Mars is sometimes called the Red Planet because from Earth it looks red. For centuries people have associated the color of Mars with war.

Does Mars's red color carry a message of war, though—or is it red for another, less worrying reason?

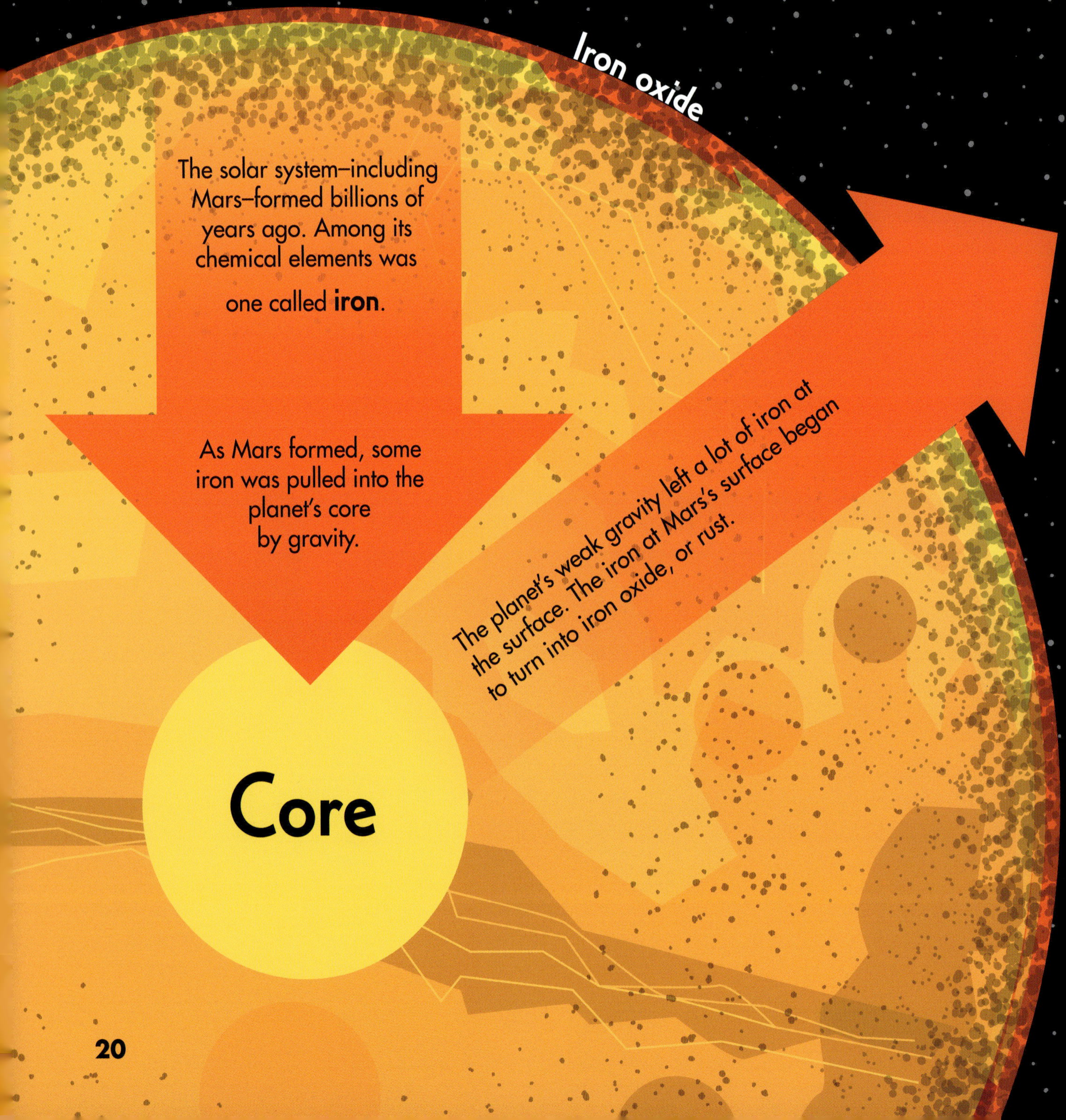

The iron oxide was blown into the atmosphere by massive volcanic eruptions. It finally settled across practically the whole planet.

Mars' biggest volcano, **Olympus Mons**, is 13 miles (21 km) high.

When light hits the layer of iron oxide, blue and green colors are absorbed. Red, though, is reflected back. This is why when you look at Mars, it seems red.

If Mars' red color is a signal from warlike aliens hoping to invade Earth, we need to be worried. In space terms, Mars isn't very far away!

Fortunately, there are no aliens on Mars. In fact, probes sent from Earth have found there is no life at all.

Risky Ride to Neptune

Neptune is the planet furthest from the sun. It's a really long way away–at least 2.6 million miles (4.3 billion km).

Using a current spacecraft, it would take about 10 1/2 years to get to Neptune. Fortunately, there would be plenty to look at on the way, but the journey also contains many potential dangers.

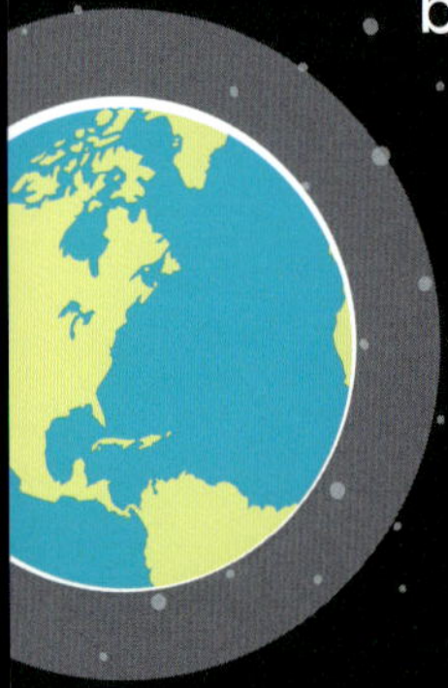

The first planet you pass is Mars. Hopefully you won't end up like Mars' two moons. They were once asteroids, but got caught in Mars's gravity and couldn't leave!

As your spacecraft passes through the Asteroid Belt, be careful not to crash. Even a small collision would spell catastrophe.

Jupiter is two-and-a-half times the size of all the other planets put together. Steer clear–Jupiter's gravity is strong! You wouldn't want to be pulled into the Great Red Spot: a violent storm so huge that three Earths could fit inside it.

Uranus is a freezing ice giant. It looks blue because of the stinky methane gas in its atmosphere. Below the methane, violent storms constantly rage.

Like Jupiter, Saturn is a gas giant. Its most amazing feature is its rings, which are made mostly of ice. A giant chunk of ice could do some serious damage to your spacecraft!

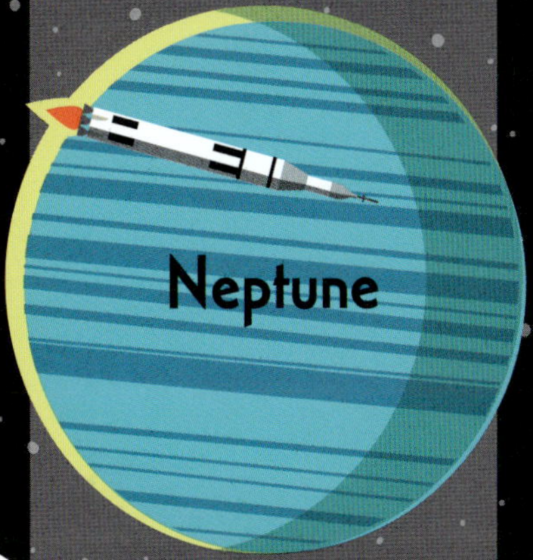

Once you reach Neptune, you might want to come right home again! Neptune is not exactly a tourist destination: it's freezing cold and constantly whipped by winds of over 1,200 miles (2,000 km) per hour. No visitor could survive down there.

Death of a Star

Stars get their energy from hydrogen in their core. Eventually, that hydrogen is used up.

Bigger, brighter stars use up their hydrogen more quickly than smaller ones. But whatever its size, a star's hydrogen always runs out in the end.

As the **hydrogen** runs out, the star swells up and glows more brightly. It becomes a red giant.

When the sun eventually becomes a red giant (in about 5 billion years), Earth will be toast!

The star's fuel finally runs out.

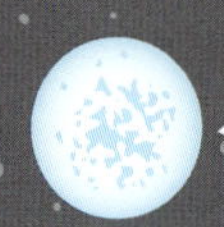

With ordinary stars, a layer of gas explodes outwards and the core cools down. It becomes a white dwarf.

When a giant star's fuel runs out, it collapses inwards. The star's matter bounces off its core, producing a massive ...

supernova explosion!

Supernovas produce more light than a whole galaxy of normal stars–but only for about a month.

After, only the core of the supernova is left. It has such strong gravity that even light cannot escape. It becomes a black hole.

Black holes have an imaginary line around them called the event horizon. Once something passes the event horizon, it is impossible to escape the black hole's gravity.

Great Balls of Fire!

At the heart of our galaxy is a massive black hole. Once in a while, it spits out a star. The star, a giant, flaming ball of gas, crashes through the universe.

But what causes this to happen?

The black hole has very strong gravity and is constantly pulling in space matter.

Sometimes the black hole pulls in two stars that are in orbit around each other. They are like dancers holding hands, spinning around.

As the stars are sucked towards the black hole, its gravity adds to the speed of their spinning.

Eventually the stars spin so fast that they cannot stay together. It's as if the dancers have suddenly let go.

One star is sucked into the black hole. The other is flung away at high speed.

The star travels out of the galaxy at millions of miles per hour.

It keeps going until it hits something or runs out of energy and becomes a white dwarf.

If a star like this came our way, life on Earth (and Earth itself) would cease to exist.

Fortunately, we would see such a star coming a long way off. Astronomers would probably know a few centuries ahead of time and hopefully come up with a plan!

The Galactic Cannibals

Did you know that galaxies can "eat" each other? This process has the brilliant name: galactic cannibalism.

Galactic cannibalism starts when a small galaxy is close to a much bigger galaxy.

Big galaxies have very strong gravity. This gravity pulls on smaller galaxies nearby.

The smaller galaxy is slowly drawn towards the cannibal.

When the small galaxy gets close enough, its own gravity can no longer hold its stars and planets in place. They start to be attracted by the cannibal galaxy instead.

The small galaxy slowly breaks up and becomes part of the bigger galaxy.

It takes billions of years for one galaxy to eat another.

Unfortunately, our galaxy, the Milky Way, has a **MUCH** bigger next-door neighbor: Andromeda.

Andromeda has already smashed into and eaten at least one other galaxy, maybe more. And Andromeda is heading our way at 185 miles (300 km) per second.

When Andromeda arrives it will cause galactic chaos. The whole Milky Way will be wrecked!

Fortunately, Andromeda won't be arriving for about a billion years.

Glossary

air lock small space with doors at opposite sides, so one door can be shut and sealed before the other is opened

astronomer person who studies the planets, stars, and other celestial bodies

celestial body any natural space object that can be seen by astronomers

chemical element basic chemical unit which cannot be broken down into something else

chemical reaction process of substances changing into something else, such as metal rusting or wood burning

contaminant polluting or poisonous substance

density describes how tightly packed the inside of an object is

gas giant large planet made mainly of gas

gravity force of attraction of an object. Gravity depends on an object's size, with greater size producing more gravity.

ice giant large planet made mainly of frozen matter

jettison cast off or away

lunar module landing craft for visiting the moon's surface

meteor meteoroid (a piece of space rock) that falls into Earth's atmosphere

meteorite meteor that hits Earth's surface

moon orbit curved path around the moon

nauseous feeling sick, as though wanting to vomit

orbit circular path around another object, where the object's gravity and your own speed are in balance

radiate spread outwards

red giant star that has swelled and glows red after its supply of hydrogen has run out

resource useable supply of something, such as water, air, or food

syndrome group of medical symptoms

tether cord or strap used to hold an object in place. In gravity-free space, tethers come in very handy.

white dwarf small, very dense star

zero-G short for "zero gravity"

Finding Out More

Books

Lombardo, Jennifer. *The James Webb Space Telescope.* Buffalo, NY: PowerKids Press, 2025.

van der Veken, Jan. *Space: From Sputnik to the International Space Station.* New York, NY: Prestel, 2024.

Websites

NASA Space Place
https://spaceplace.nasa.gov/
Explore so much of space on this site.

Passport to Space
https://kids.nationalgeographic.com/space
Check out more about space and play games here.

Index

Aldrin, Buzz 12–13
Andromeda 29
animals 9
Apollo 11 12–13
Armstrong, Neil 12–13
Asteroid Belt 22
asteroids 10, 22
astronauts 12–19
astronomers 27

black holes 25–27

cannibalism, galactic 28–29
Collins, Michael 12–13
comets 10
command module 13

dinosaurs 11

Earth 5, 7–16, 19–22, 24, 27
eclipses, total 9
energy 6–7, 24, 27
extra vehicular activity (EVA) 18–19

galaxies 25–29
gas giants 22–23
Giant Red Spot 22–23
gravity 12, 14–16, 19–20, 22, 25–26, 28

horizon, event 25
hydrogen 24

ice giants 23
International Space Station 17
iron/iron oxide 20–21

jet pack 19
Jupiter 22–23

lunar module 13

Mars 20–22
meteorites 10–11
meteoroids 10
meteors 10–11, 19
Milky Way 29
moon 8–9, 12–14

Neptune 22–23

Olympus Mons 21

photosphere 6
plants 7–8

red giants 24–25
Red Planet 20–21
rockets, space 12–13

Saturn 23
solar flares 6–7
solar system 6, 20–23
space stations 14–19
space walks 18–19
spacecraft 12–19, 22–23
stars 6, 10, 24–28
sun 5–9, 22, 24
supernovas 25

Uranus 23
Urine Processing Assembly 17

volcanoes 21

weather 7–8
white dwarf 24, 27

zero-G 16